AF397248

HER MELANIN, HER SKIN

by

David Kamali

First edition, 2021

Cover illustration: iStock.com/Ponomariova_Maria

Förlag: BoD – Books on Demand, Stockholm, Sverige

Tryck: BoD – Books on Demand, Norderstedt, Tyskland

ISBN 978-91-7969-158-5

To Her,
I Hope This Book Finds You.

FOREWORD

I WAS thirteen years old when I wrote my first poem. I remember the hype and simple joy that it created in me. I rushed into the living room and read it out loud. When I finished, my brother laughed at me and said that it was the "most horrible" poem he had ever heard, but my mom took me aside, kissed my forehead, and told me that I would be a great poet and writer one day. She then took my faulty poem and put it in her photo album.

Some months ago, my student sent me his short story. It was a superb story, with colourful imagery and beautiful similes. I saw myself in him, the same young passionate kid who tried eagerly to do good but always feared it would not be enough. I had a conversation with him, and I told him the exact thing my mom told me some years ago. I sowed a seed of faith, hoping that the seed will grow and become a sequoia one day. It was then, I truly realised the power of words, and I decided to write and complete this poetry collection.

When I first started writing this poetry collection, I feared deeply that my emotions would not give way to the impact this book intended to have on you. It took me a while to overcome that fear, to make a decision and to start the process. During the process of writing *Her Melanin, Her Skin,*

I realised that we humans are incredibly flawed and we try earnestly to see the flaws of others while hiding our own. I realised that loving a person truly is not a feeling but a decision. It is a decision to accept the other person with whatever flaws they have, whatever mistakes they had made, and whatever path they take. I realised that loving is a process, and every process takes time. It requires energy, communication, and patience.

It took me months to bring to life everything that had happened. Even though I had to change some names and events, I stayed true to the story, to myself, and to you as the reader. I believe that all of us have a story, but many of us do not dare to share it. I hope that my story connects to yours and becomes an inspiration for you to write your own.

The Author

CONTENTS

CHAPTER I

WE

Me,
We,
The only way
We can
Be.

Chapter II

Visible

A seagull in the sky,
A grey dog in the corner of the street,
A little boy on his bicycle,
A pigeon on the edge of my balcony,
A Cuban cigar,
With its dark brown style
And its blue smoke,
Visible.
A broken heart,
Not visible.
Me, myself, and I,
Visible.

CHAPTER III

MIRACLE

She told me not to tell you,
I told her that I will.
She tore my heart to pieces,
It's a miracle standing still.

She was mine and I was hers,
No boundaries between us.
We laughed, we talked, we smiled.
I remember it as it was.

A wave came crashing down,
It destroyed everything.
She told me not to tell you
The lonely nights that I sing.

Chapter IV

Set You Free

"It is not you love, it's just me."
"Stop this lie! Stop this!"
"I promise, it is just me."
"The truth will set you free."

"I'm sorry I have to pack!"
"Sorry won't heal anything."
"What would you want me to do?"
"Can you give me my time back?"

"That, my dear, I can't do."
"You lied to me you called me *boo*."
"I'm sorry but I'm leaving now!"
"One day you will miss me, too."

Chapter V

Tears

She left the keys and ran outside.
She took the cab without good-bye.

That
Damned
Yellow
Cab.
Why
Didn't
She
Look
Back?

Tears
Ran.

My room,
Larger than ever.

"God,
Help me to pick up the pieces
Of my shattered
heart."
The space of emptiness,
Is vast.
Loneliness
Lasts.

Tears
Stopped.

I found a letter on my bed.
It was hers.
I wish,
It wasn't.
I read it aloud,
My sound
Echoed.

"I'm sorry that I left you,
So sorry that I hurt you!
You helped me
To survive my darkest times,
You had the finest heart.
You wiped my tears
When I cried,
And I never asked
Why!
I'm sorry but I'm not yours,
You healed my heart

And I hurt yours.
But the thing is
That I can't
Be with
You
Anymore.
You
Deserve
Better."

Tears
Ran.

I
Deserve
You.

Chapter VI

Soul

I met her at the bus stop,
On a cold February morning,
Two days before
Valentine's Day.

High heels,
Blue jeans,
Yellow dress,
Blue denim jacket.
Her beautiful
Afro hair.
Rose
Lipsticks,
Shining.
Her melanin
Popping.
My heart
Bouncing.

Breathtaking.

So take a deep breath!

Empty sits,
I was standing.
My algebra book,
Burdened my back,
I didn't mind.
I wanted to see her.

I
Saw
Her.
She
Saw
Me.
We
Smiled.

"You can sit here
If you want?!"
"May I?"
"Oh,
So polite."
"I…
I…
You
Are
Gorgeous."
"Huh,

What's your name, silly?"
"You can call me Dave."

"Nice to meet you,
Dave.
I'm
Soul."

Chapter VII

Whole

Soul,
Whole.

Chapter VIII

Wink

"Soul,
Can I
See you again?"
"Come and see me
The day after tomorrow.
And bring me
A white
Flower.
And
Maybe some
White chocolate too."

Wink.

A pen.
Her number.
My hand.

CHAPTER IX

NEXT STATION

We separated at
Train station.
Next station,
My heart.
Train number,
Love O one.

CHAPTER X

HER

Her Melanin,
Her Skin.
Blazing.
Amazing.

Chapter XI

First Sight

They lied to us.
Those who said
"Love at first sight
Does not exist."

Just look at God!
He fell in love with us,
The moment
He formed us.

Chapter XII

A Soft Kiss

The lamppost
Shined its light
And invited
The old insects
To an unknown reunion.

"I'm outside" text
Was delivered
Five minutes ago.
Read
Three minutes ago.

No answers.

Anxiety tried to creep in.
Push it out!
Push it out!
She is coming.

I can feel her.
She can
Feel me.

The moon tried hard
To reflect its friend's light
But failed
To illuminate the darkness
Of this city.

My eyes
Were fastened to the stairway
Of the cold apartment
Through its old window,
Fuggy,
A February night,
No sign of light.

My ears
Were ready for a small sound of hope.
Hope,
A strong desire,
A dangerous impulse.

Then I heard
The sound of her footsteps.
Humane.
A white flower,
Cold and Wet,
Was freezing to death,
Only shouting:

"I belong to the ground."

In her hands,
A box of white chocolate.
Opened immediately.
Shared.
Eaten.
Finished.
A soft kiss.
Hands in Hands.
The cold February Friday night
Was getting warmer.
Destination,
My apartment.

Chapter XIII

Her Lips

Her lips,
On my cheeks.
My lips
Whispering.
"You are flawless,
Stay tonight!"

Her hands
Surrounded me.
My hands,
On her waist.
"Dance with me!"
Jazz in the background.

Her gentle skin,
Touched.
Her melanin,
Felt.

Her breath,
Breathed.
Her heartbeat,
Heard.

The wind
Knocked on my window.
Let me in.
Let me be
With her.
Alone.

Chapter XIV

Her Melanin, Her Skin

Her melanin,
Her skin.
Her melanin,
My skin.
Her body,
My flesh.
Her heart,
My soul.
United.

Chapter XV

Mount Zion

Awake. 6 a.m.
Bread dancing in the warm oven,
Canned tuna and egg,
Dried fruit, peanut butter and jelly. Goofy voice:
"Excuse me, ma'am.
Follow me, please!"
"Grow up!" said she, laughing,
"How did you sleep?"
"It was like heaven, the space between your arms."
Jazz gave his place to blues,
King, B.B. The Thrill is Gone.
"Let's eat. I'm starving."
"Me, too. But hold on! Kiss me first!"
No question asked.
On the bed, I kissed her.
Proud.
Quiet.
Remember!

She is yours,
Truly.
Unreachable is now reached.
Victorious, Together.
We are
Xerxes and Esther. Grateful.
You are my Mount
Zion. Strong. Stable.

Chapter XVI

A Touch of Poetry

She was looking around,
A girl with curiosity.

There was a bed,
King-size,
Made for a soldier.
Two light brown chairs,
One for me,
One in case.
She was the case
That day
And days to come.
A table,
White,
Stable.
A lamp,
Bright.
A drawer

Full of clothes
Eager to cover nakedness,
Only to realise that
Nakedness
Is not only external
But internal, too.

A bookshelf,
One side English books,
Novels mostly
And a touch of poetry.
Gibran Khalil Gibran,
Gwendolyn Brooks,
Pablo Neruda,
Rumi.
The other side,
Mathematics.
She touched
My Calculus book,
Opened it up,
Read two sentences,
Closed it and put it back.
"You a smart one, aren't you?"
I laughed.
"Can you teach me, Mr. teacher?"
"Can you nurse me, Ms. nurse?"

Chapter XVII

Input

"I can tell you one thing;
Life is a math equation
With unknown variables.
Different.
Unpredictable.
The end result
Depends on your input."

Chapter XVIII

A Gun, No Magazine.

Again,
She examined my place.
A wooden cross
On the wall.
A dried rose
That used to be
Bright and red
As I recall.

A worn-out Bible,
Seated
Near a pair of
Glasses
Ready to be read.

A picture of my childhood.

A boy with a smile
And a simple style.
Happy,
Sad within.

A gun,
No magazine,
Screwed to the wall.
Old,
Workable.
Used,
Not anymore.

"Why do you keep a gun?"
"It is a reminder of my past."
"Were you a bad man, Dave?"
"I knew you would've asked at last."

"Tell me!"

"I made a lot of bad choices.
I was broken,
But now
Healed.
I was angry,
But now
Still.
I was empty,
But now
Fulfilled.

Chapter XIX

Look Past the Past

She took her bag,
A pilgrim in my shrine
Ready for departure.
"I'm working the whole week,
Late-night shifts."
"Then I'll meet you next week,
Maybe pizza and a movie?"
"Okay.
Can you call me a cab?"

I followed her outside,
The cold wind followed me.
The cab driver
Was searching,
Confused.
She waved,
He nodded,
And turned his car around.

She hugged me.
Her hands,
Covered my head.
Her fingers,
Combed my long hair.
I closed my eyes.
The scent of her ZARA perfume,
Echoed in my nose.
I remembered the taste of
Her lips.
Last night,
We became
One.

"I always look past the past, Dave."
A kiss on my lips,
Steady but fast,
Soft,
Tranquil,
Reassuring me,
She was real.

She opened the car's door,
And looked back.
"SUSHI"
"What?"
"I want sushi,
not pizza."
She smiled.

So that was what happiness
Looked like.

Chapter XX

I Hate Good-byes

No good-byes?
Good.
I hate good-byes.
See you later,
Sounds better.

CHAPTER XXI

KING JR.

I met her at her place.
Small,
Cosy,
One bedroom.
Eiffel Tower key-chain,
On the desk.
Her nurse name tag,
Beside it.

A queen-size bed,
Worthy of her majesty.
A small kitchen.
Some Chinese food
In the refrigerator.
A table,
A mirror,
A chair,
And her.

A poster with written words:

A painting of Martin Luther King Jr.
On the wall,
A true legend, a star
In a crowd of a million.
Ministering and leading
A whole generation to
A brighter future,
A very near future,
A future yet to come.

Maybe in another life,
I would have held your hand,
Tight,
Together,
We would march to Washington,
With millions of men
Watching.
But tonight,
I would hold your hand,
Tight,
Together,
We would march to your bed,
With millions of stars
Watching
From the sky above
Stockholm.

"We are a product
Of his dream."
"We indeed are.
Free at last!
Free to love."
"Hold me tight!"

CHAPTER XXII

SUSHI

I sat on the bed,
She sat on the chair.
I drew the table near,
She drew me near.
We were
Close.

The smell of
Soy sauce,
Wasabi,
And shrimp
Perfumed the air.
She started eating.
I failed.
"I can't eat with these!
I need a fork."
She laughed.
"Here,

Let me help you."
She held the chopstick
Perfectly.
She took a bite,
I took a bite.
Back and forth.
It tasted
Different,
The sushi,
It tasted
Love.

Chapter XXIII

Her Afro Hair

We lay down
On her bed.
Her bed,
Brown.
Two lovers
In the town.

My left hand,
Her pillow.
My right hand,
Her cover.
My body,
Her luxury blanket.

She turned to me,
Face to face.
I could feel her breath,
Warm.

Her heartbeat,
Loud.
Her Afro hair,
Soft.
Her soul,
Light.

I could see her eyes,
Dark. Bright.
Her teeth,
White.
I could hear her voice,
Polite.

My lips
Touched her lips.

Her lips
Set a fire
In my soul.
Her hands
Drew me close.
My heart
Heard her heart.
My body
Kissed hers.
Eyes closed,
Hearts opened,
Lights out.

Chapter XXIV

Candle

Her birthday came in May.
A new chapter,
25 rounds around the sun.
I bought her a golden necklace,
A small cross attached to it.
It was just me
Her,
Us,
No one else.
We against the world.
We were made for each other.
"Are you gonna buy me a ring, too?"
She laughed.
I laughed, too.
"Maybe I will."
"Maybe you should."

The cork

Was pulled.
The wine
Was poured.

The flame told the candle:
"In order to shine bright
You need to burn
Deep."

"Make a wish, my love!"
"I did.
You're already here."

The candle
Was blown.

Chapter XXV

The Meaning of Life

She put her soft lips near my ear.
"Dave,
Are you awake?
Dave!"
"I am now."
I smiled,
Eyes closed.
"I can't sleep,"
She whispered.
"Will you talk to me?"
I opened my eyes.
Her smile,
Wider than Nile,
Could be seen
From a mile
Away.

"Of course I will."

She put her head on my chest.
My ears,
Open for her words.
Ready to receive,
Ready to believe.

"Do you think I am old?"
"Age
Is what we define it to be."
"I'm afraid."
"We fear
What we don't understand.
Sometimes,
It is complex
To understand
Life."
"I'm happy to have you,
Boo."

I kissed her head,
Gently.
The smell of coconut oil
In her soft afro hair
Anointed my soul.

"Dave?"
"Yes, babe?"
"What is the meaning of life?"
I paused a moment,

Thinking,
Seeking.

"The meaning of life
Is to do justly,
To love mercy,
To walk humbly with God,
And to love."

"I love you!"
"I love you,
Too."

Chapter XXVI

Seconds

Seconds
Gave birth to minutes.
Minutes gave birth to hours.
Hours gave birth to days.
Days turned to weeks,
Weeks to months,
And nobody could stop the cycle.
There was only one way.
To expect it,
To respect it,
To accept it.

CHAPTER XXVII

HIM

I was home,
That warm afternoon.
The sound of boiling water
Disturbed the peace of the room.
I tolerated it,
For the reward was a warm cup of coffee.

I sipped my coffee.
Oh the taste of
Sweetness and saltiness.
Perfection. Toffee.

I read through my Number Theory book,
And tried to find
The greatest common divisor
Of 252 and 198.
"Wait! It's 18.
Great.

Too easy."

I heard the sound of a key
Turning in my lock.
She rushed in,
Crying.
She held me,
Tight.

The black rivers on her cheeks,
A mixture of tears and mascara,
Drowned me.

"What is wrong, Soul?"
My tears,
Crossed the borders of my eyes.
I
Burst into tears.
My soul
Burst into flames.
Her sadness,
My sadness.

"I saw him,
In the park,
On my way home.
He was
Walking his damn dog.
He was out!"

"Who?"

"Him."
"*Him?*"
"HIM!"

"My love…"
"My face still hurts
Because of his fists."

She sobbed,
Bitterly.

"You are with me now.
You are
Safe.
I will
Protect you.
I promise!"

She cried with fears,
I feared her tears.

Chapter XXVIII

Raised by a Woman

Any man
Who raises his hand
On a woman
Has not been raised by a woman.

Chapter XXIX

Silence

Darkness cannot drive out darkness;
Only light can do that.
Hate cannot drive out hate;
Only love can do that.
Silence cannot drive out silence;
Only words can do that.

"Talk to me,
My love."
"I feel broken."
"You are bent,
But never broken."

Chapter XXX

Proud. Strong.

"Keep your head up.
Let the sun shine upon you.
Let them see your face.
Proud,
Stable,
Strong.

The shadows
Will be left behind
Once you turn to the sun.

Show them!
The power of your beauty,
The power of your melanin."

CHAPTER XXXI

BARE SOUL

I was making breakfast
When she woke up.
I went to her.
"Sorry for yesterday."
"Don't ever apologise
For being you.
I love the way you are.
Don't just give me your bare body,
Give me your bare soul,
Soul,
In this naked world.

Just be yourself,
Others
Are already
Taken."

Chapter XXXII

Lunch

She locked her hands
Behind my back.
Eye contact,
Deep stare.
She kissed me.
We made love.
Breakfast
Became
Lunch.

Chapter XXXIII

Ice Cream

Her hands
In mine.

A gentle kiss on my lips.

She started to laugh.
"Wipe that lipstick off!"
I wiped off the lipstick,
Even though
I didn't want to.
I was marked
By her.

"Let me buy you an ice cream, Soul."
"Okay, love.
But let's share one.
I want blueberry.
Now,

You choose one!"
"Grapefruit!"
"What about dark chocolate?
Your favourite."
"I've already tasted
The tastiest
Dark chocolate
In the world.
No desire left."

She smiled.
"I love you,
My goofy white chocolate."

A gentle kiss on my lips.

CHAPTER XXXIV

SANDCASTLE

The kindness of the sun,
The joy of children,
The moisture of the air.
God,
With his majestic hands,
Painted the clouds.

The sky,
A blue heaven,
Sang a soundless song.

A child
Was building a sandcastle,
Ignorant of the fact
That the waves
Would be his enemies
In a few hours,
Even though

They were disguised
As allies
Who kindly
Touched his feet
And ran back
To the never-ending sea.

Grains of golden sands,
On her beautiful
Black skin,
Begged to join
Their home,
The beach.

Her gentle hand,
Softer than river sand,
Kept me close.
Me,
Speechless.
She,
Sleepless.
Her fingers
Chained mine.
Her closed eyes
Tamed mine.

I was
But a prisoner
Whose prison
Was within,
Willingly

Staying.

A prisoner of love,
Free at last.
Free at last.

"Can I be your lover?
Forever?"
I murmured.
Her sleeplessness
Had taken her
To the abyss.
She was there.
She wasn't there.
She was
Asleep.

Chapter XXXV

Paris

I booked us a trip,
A weekend in Paris.
A selfie with the Eiffel Tower,
A visit to the Louvre,
A kiss on the Pont Neuf.

City lights,
Rooftop bars,
Memories,
Good old
Memories.

CHAPTER XXXVI

OUR HEARTS

We came back,
But our hearts
Stayed there
For a while.

Chapter XXXVII

Couple Goals

Long walks near the beach,
Salad bars,
Sunset near the shore.

Chill vibes,
Chilly nights.
I,
Giving her my jacket,
She,
Giving me her hugs.

Movie theatre,
Small fear of getting caught
For sneaking in
Home-made popcorn.

Silly poses on camera,
Friends saying

"Couple goals".
We were in a different
Dimension.

Chapter XXXVIII

Our First Silly Little Fight

We took the train
An August night.
The night was starry
And outside was bright.
She was my queen
And I was her knight.
She asked for a poem
I said: "I'd rather write.
But I warn you
The chance is slight
That I write a good poem
which I can recite."
I was nervous
And my head felt light.
I spilt my coffee
And her shirt was white.

She got mad
But said: "It's alright."
We laughed, and I named my poem
Our first silly little fight.

Chapter XXXIX

A Daughter

I put my head on her shoulder.
The 6-hour trip
Was about to end.
Two nights in Copenhagen
Were about to begin.
Every end is a beginning.

"Dave,
If God gives you a daughter,
What advice would you give her?"

"I would tell her
To give her heart
Only to true love.

I would tell her:
'My daughter,
If you expect a good harvest,

Sow a good seed.
If you expect love,
Sow love.
If you expect success,
Sow with effort.
If you expect generosity,
Sow in abundance.
If you expect change,
Sow differently.'

I would tell her
That she should
Listen to her mother
And that I will always
Love her."

CHAPTER XL

A SON

"Dave,
If God gives you a son,
What advice would you give him?"

"I would tell him
That success
Is a choice.
So make that choice
Today!

I would teach him:
'My son,
Always love your mother,
Always be polite.
Always respect women.
Always be a gentleman.
Never break a promise.
And never break a heart.'

I would tell him
That he should
Listen to his mother
And that I will always
Love him."

Chapter XLI

A Great Father

"You will be a great dad
One day."

"You think so?"

"I believe so."

"I don't know.
I'm human,
I'm flawed.
I'm not a saint,
Just a sinner.
I'm not a king
Just a soldier.
I'm not perfect
Just a man full of mistakes."

"And you still

Can love.
That is what you're
Made of.
Remember,
Your path
Is shaped
By your steps.
And your steps
Were shaped by your mistakes.
You will make a great father
Someday.
One day."

CHAPTER XLII

GREW IN LOVE

That night in the hotel room,
My fingers
Ran on her naked body,
Smoothly,
Feeling her melanin,
Slowly.

"Have you fallen in love with me, Dave?"
"I haven't.
If I fall in love with you
I can fall out of love.
I grew in love
With you."

My kisses,
Her lips.
They encountered each other,
Again.

Round two.

Chapter XLIII

No Regrets

I loved waking up next to her.
No fears.
No regrets.

Chapter XLIV

My Home

No train,
A direct flight,
A cab from Arlanda.
Home sweet home.

My home is
Where she is.

Chapter XLV

Streets of New York

My thoughts
Were busier than the
Streets of New York.
My body,
London.
My mind,
The Underground.
Crowded as usual.

I cannot sleep.
I have to think
Deep.
I will tell her tomorrow.

"Tell me what?"
She said,

With a faint voice.
"Nothing, love.
I was thinking out loud.
Let's sleep."

Chapter XLVI

Marry You

"I want to
Marry you."
"I…
I can't, Dave."
"Tell me
Why?"
"I…
I don't deserve you.
I don't deserve your love.
You deserve better."
"I DESERVE YOU."

Silence.
Just silence.
The loudest sound ever made.

"Soul,
Let me

Hold
You!"

"No!
I have to
Go."

Chapter XLVII

You

She called a cab,
She packed her bag.
I should have known,
It was a red flag.

Without you,
I don't know who
I am.
I don't know whose
I am.

Chapter XLVIII

Seasons

They said:
"Life is a journey through seasons."
Then
Why is my winter
So long.

CHAPTER XLIX

MY EVERYTHING

Rumi said:
"Lose yourself,
Lose yourself in this love.
When you lose yourself in this love,
You will find everything."

The fact is
I found myself,
Found myself in this love.
When I found myself in this love,
I lost everything.

She was
My everything.

CHAPTER L

YELLOW CAB

That damned
Yellow cab!

I dropped the letter
On my bed.
The only time
I felt all my emotions
Worked together
Hand in hand,
Merged,
Meld,
Shared.

Cold water
Splashed from shower head
On my shoulders.
Cold,
Like a good-bye kiss

On a winter night.

I don't remember
If it was the water
Or my tears
That washed me clean that day.

CHAPTER LI

GOOD-BYE

23:37

"Hey.
This is Soul.
Sorry I can't take your call.
Please
Leave your name and number,
And I will call you
As soon as possible."
Beep

Another try!
Maybe she answers
This time.

"Hey.
This is Soul.
Sorry I can't take your call.

Please
Leave your name and number,
And I will call you
As soon as possible."
Beep
"Hey soul.
I called like ten times.
I just
Wanted to hear
Your voice.

I kinda did.

Um...

Good-bye."

I HATE GOOD-BYES.

Chapter LII

A Damn Lie

They said:
"Time heals."

It's a damn lie.
Time doesn't heal
Anything.
It just
Covers the pain.

CHAPTER LIII

ALL I HAD

Everything I said
Taunted me.
Everything I wrote
Haunted me.
Everything I thought
Judged me.
Everything I heard,
Mocked me.

Everything I read,
Knocked me
Down.
Everything I felt
Caused me
Pain.

You were
Whom I saw.

You were
What I wrote.
You were
What I heard.
You were
All I had.

Chapter LIV

Scar

I've realised by far
No wounds heal without a scar.

Chapter LV

This World

They said:
"You get what you ask for
In this world."

I asked for love.
I got
Nothing.

Chapter LVI

Purpose

For living,
A purpose is required.
For a while,
My purpose
Was to love you.

CHAPTER LVII

A POET WITHOUT A POEM

What is a man without love?

I should know.

Maybe it is a boy
Without a father,
Raised by a single mother,
Beaten by an unloving brother.

I should know.

What is a poet without a poem?

I should know.

Maybe it is a man,

left alone
By the one
He truly loved
And longed for.

I should know.

CHAPTER LVIII

NONE

What is a man without love?
What is a boy without a dad?
What is a poet without a poem?
What is happy without sad?

Non-being,
Nullity,
Nobody,
Empty,
None,
Who,
Me,
I.

CHAPTER LIX

YOUR MELANIN, YOUR SKIN

A seagull in the sky
Shouting for a mate.
A grey dog in the corner of the street
Protecting her territory
From invisible enemies.

A little boy on his bicycle
Pretending he owns a motorcycle,
Shouting:
"Vroom, Vroom".

A pigeon on the edge of my balcony
Not moving,
Scanning me with its red eye.

A Cuban cigar,

With its dark brown style
And its blue smoke,
Visible.
Was it I who smoked the cigar,
Or was it the cigar that smoked me?

A broken heart,
Not visible.
Was it I who broke the heart,
Or was it the heart that broke me?

Bling
A text message received:
"I miss YOU!"
From
Her.

I didn't know
How a simple text
Can heal a broken heart.

"I …
I …
I miss you, too."
Delete!
DELETE!

A missed phone call,
From her.
Again.

Bling
Another text message.
"Babe,
I'm sorry.
I was just
Afraid.
I need you.
I want you.
I love you.
Truly.
Believe me!"

Ignored.
Again.

Bling
"Do you still love me?"

I cannot ignore,
Not anymore.

"I will always love you.
Nothing can change that!
I miss you, too.
I miss your everything.
Your voice,
Your eyes,
Your smile,
Your melanin,
Your skin."

Sending…
Pending…
Sent.

CHAPTER LX

SECOND CHANCE

Every second chance
Is a new beginning.

Afterword

For the first time I met her, I knew she was the one I always desired. Our story briefly matched, but it was not in the right season. We were young, and we rushed it. A seed needs time to grow. A relationship needs to be in the right season with the right person. If it is the right season, but with the wrong person, your heart will be broken. If it is the wrong season and but with the right person, their heart will be broken. It is, however, good to make mistakes. You learn to be patient, trust the process, let go and let God take control. Growth and maturity do not come from making mistakes, but from learning from them.

In short, it has been an extraordinary process to write this poetry collection, and it is hoped that it has been pleasant to read. Acknowledgement must be made to those without whom this book would have never been completed.

I genuinely hope that my inspirational book has touched your passionate heart.

Sincerely,
David Kamali
June 2021